INTRODUCTION

Retiring early is a dream that many aspire to but few achieve. The allure of financial independence, the freedom to pursue passions, and the ability to spend time with loved ones without the constraints of a 9-to-5 job are enticing prospects. In a world where the traditional retirement age often seems distant, the idea of leaving the workforce years, or even decades, early is both exhilarating and achievable with the right mindset and planning.

This book is designed to guide you on the journey to early retirement, providing practical strategies, insights, and inspiration to help you break free from the conventional retirement timeline. We will explore the foundational principles of financial independence, the various approaches within the FIRE (Financial Independence, Retire Early) movement, and actionable steps you can take to reshape your financial future.

Understanding your current financial situation is crucial, as it serves as the starting point for your journey. Throughout this book, we will emphasize the importance of setting clear financial goals, creating a frugal budget, and developing multiple streams of income. By focusing on these key elements, you can build a robust financial foundation that supports your dream of early retirement.

In addition to practical advice, we will address the emotional and psychological aspects of transitioning to retirement. Achieving financial independence is not just about numbers; it's about envisioning the life you want to lead and finding fulfillment outside of traditional work.

Whether you're just beginning to think about early retirement or are already on the path, this book will provide you with the tools and knowledge you need to make informed decisions. As you read on, remember that the journey to early retirement is not a sprint but a marathon, and every step you take brings you closer to your goal. Let's embark on this journey together and explore how you can make the dream of retiring early a reality.

CHAPTER 1: UNDERSTANDING EARLY RETIREMENT

Defining Early Retirement

Early retirement is generally defined as leaving the workforce significantly earlier than the traditional retirement age, which is often considered to be around 65. While the exact age may vary depending on individual circumstances, many people who pursue early retirement aim to do so in their 30s, 40s, or early 50s. This goal is not just about the age at which one stops working; it encompasses achieving financial independence and the freedom to live life on one's own terms.

The benefits of retiring early are numerous and impactful. One of the most appealing advantages is the opportunity for a more fulfilling life. By freeing yourself from the daily grind of a full-time job, you gain the time and flexibility to explore your passions, travel, and spend quality time with family and friends. Early retirement can also lead to reduced stress and improved mental health, as the pressures of work and financial insecurity are alleviated. Additionally, having more time allows for personal growth, whether that means pursuing new hobbies, continuing education, or volunteering in your community.

Despite the many benefits, early retirement is often shrouded in misconceptions. A common belief is that it requires immense wealth or a high-paying job. While financial stability is essential, achieving early retirement is more about strategic planning, disciplined saving, and smart investing than it is about earning a large income. Another misconception is that retiring early means completely abandoning work. In reality, many who retire early choose to engage in part-time work, pursue entrepreneurial ventures, or dedicate time to meaningful projects that bring them joy and fulfillment.

Understanding what early retirement truly means is the first step on the path to achieving this goal. It requires not only a clear financial strategy but also a vision for how you want to spend your time once you have the freedom to choose. As you navigate this journey, keep in mind that early retirement is as much about mindset and lifestyle as it is about finances.

Benefits Of Retiring Early

Retiring early offers a myriad of benefits that can significantly enhance your quality of life. One of the most immediate advantages is the gift of time. With the traditional work schedule behind you, you can allocate your days to pursuits that truly matter to you—whether that's spending more time with family, traveling to new destinations, or diving into hobbies you've always wanted to explore. This newfound freedom allows for a richer, more fulfilling life experience.

Another key benefit is improved mental and physical well-being. The stress and pressures associated with full-time employment can take a toll on your health. Early retirement can provide a welcome reprieve, leading to lower levels of anxiety and a greater sense of peace. With more time to focus on self-care, exercise, and healthy eating, many find that their overall health improves significantly after leaving the workforce.

Financial independence is also a major perk of early retirement. By strategically saving and investing during your working years, you can create a stable income stream that allows you to live comfortably without a paycheck. This financial security can lead to reduced financial stress, enabling you to focus on enjoying life rather than worrying about money.

Moreover, retiring early opens the door to personal growth and exploration. With time on your side, you can pursue educational opportunities, volunteer for causes you care about, or even start a new business based on your passions. This exploration not only enriches your life but can also foster a sense of purpose and fulfillment that might have been missing during your working years.

Finally, early retirement can improve your relationships. With more free time, you can cultivate deeper connections with friends and family, making lasting memories together. The flexibility to engage in social activities or simply be present for loved ones can lead to a more satisfying and enriched personal life.

In summary, the benefits of early retirement extend far beyond financial freedom. It's about creating a life that aligns with your values, pursuing passions, and fostering well-being in all aspects of your life. As you embark on this journey, consider how you can maximize these benefits to create the fulfilling retirement you envision.

Common Misconceptions About Retirement

When discussing early retirement, several misconceptions often arise that can cloud understanding and lead to hesitation. One of the most prevalent myths is that early retirement is only for the wealthy. Many believe that substantial financial resources are a prerequisite for retiring early, but this isn't necessarily true. With diligent planning, disciplined saving, and smart investing, individuals from various financial backgrounds can achieve early retirement. Strategies such as living below one's means and prioritizing savings can significantly alter one's financial trajectory.

Another common misconception is that retiring early means a complete withdrawal from work. Many assume that early retirees must abandon all forms of income-generating activities. In reality, many choose to pursue part-time work, freelance opportunities, or entrepreneurial ventures that align with their passions. This allows them to stay engaged, maintain social connections, and even supplement their income while enjoying more free time.

Some people believe that early retirement equates to a life of leisure and relaxation. While it's true that many early retirees enjoy newfound freedom, the reality can be more nuanced. Early retirement often requires individuals to find a new purpose or set of goals outside of traditional work. This can involve personal projects, travel, or community engagement. The key is that early retirees must actively create a fulfilling and meaningful life to avoid feelings of boredom or loss of identity.

Additionally, there is a misconception that early retirees will be financially unstable in their later years. While it's crucial to have a well-thought-out financial plan, many early retirees strategically manage their investments and savings to ensure long-term stability. By adopting prudent spending habits and being mindful of their financial health, they can sustain their lifestyle well into the future.

Lastly, some individuals fear that early retirement might lead to isolation or a lack of social engagement. While leaving a traditional workplace can alter one's daily social interactions, many early retirees find new communities and networks through hobbies, volunteer work, or continued education. Building connections outside of a work environment can lead to rich, fulfilling relationships.

By addressing these misconceptions, potential early retirees can approach their journey with a clearer perspective, setting realistic expectations and strategies that align with their goals. Understanding the truth behind these myths empowers individuals to take actionable steps toward achieving the retirement lifestyle they desire.

CHAPTER 2: ASSESSING YOUR FINANCIAL SITUATION

Evaluating Current Income, Expenses, And Savings

To embark on the journey toward early retirement, it's crucial to take a comprehensive look at your current financial situation. This evaluation begins with a clear understanding of your income, expenses, and savings, as these elements form the foundation of your financial health and retirement readiness.

Start by assessing your sources of income. This includes your salary, bonuses, and any side gigs or passive income streams. Document the total amount you bring in each month, as well as any variability in income, especially if you have freelance work or commissions. Understanding your income sources will help you gauge your financial stability and identify opportunities for growth, such as taking on additional projects or seeking promotions.

Next, turn your attention to your expenses. Categorize your monthly spending into fixed and variable expenses. Fixed expenses include rent or mortgage payments, utilities, and insurance, which remain consistent month to month. Variable expenses encompass groceries, dining out, entertainment, and discretionary spending, which can fluctuate. By tracking these expenses for at least a month, you can gain insight into your spending habits and pinpoint areas where you might cut back. Consider using a budgeting tool or app to help you track and categorize your expenses efficiently. These tools can provide a visual breakdown of where your money is going and make it easier to spot patterns or unnecessary spending.

Once you have a clear picture of your income and expenses, it's time to evaluate your savings. Calculate how much you have saved in various accounts, including emergency funds, retirement accounts (such as 401(k)s or IRAs), and any additional savings or investment accounts. Review the rate at which you are contributing to these accounts and assess whether it aligns with your long-term financial goals, particularly those related to early retirement. If your savings contributions feel insufficient, this evaluation process will help highlight areas where you can reallocate funds to boost savings.

A crucial part of this evaluation is determining your current savings rate—the percentage of your income that goes into savings and investments each month. A higher savings rate is key to achieving financial independence and early retirement. Ideally, you should aim for at least 20-30% of your income going into savings and investments, though many early retirees aim for even more aggressive rates, such as 50% or higher, depending on their goals and lifestyle preferences.

By completing this comprehensive evaluation of your income, expenses, and savings, you will have the data you need to make informed decisions about adjustments to your financial strategy. Whether it's cutting down on discretionary spending, increasing your savings contributions, or finding new sources of income, this thorough financial assessment sets the stage for planning and pursuing early retirement.

Understanding Net Worth And Cash Flow

To effectively plan for early retirement, it's essential to grasp the concepts of net worth and cash flow, as they provide valuable insights into your financial health and readiness.

Net worth is a snapshot of your financial standing at any given time. It is calculated by subtracting your total liabilities (what you owe) from your total assets (what you own). Your assets may include savings accounts, investments, real estate, and retirement accounts, while liabilities might encompass loans, credit card debt, and mortgages. Regularly calculating your net worth allows you to monitor your progress toward financial goals and assess how well you are building wealth over time. A growing net worth indicates that you are moving in the right direction toward achieving financial independence.

Cash flow, on the other hand, refers to the movement of money in and out of your accounts. It's vital to understand how much money you have coming in (income) compared to how much you are spending (expenses) over a specific period, usually monthly. Positive cash flow occurs when your income exceeds your expenses, while negative cash flow indicates that you are spending more than you earn. Maintaining positive cash flow is crucial for building savings and investing for retirement. By tracking your cash flow, you can identify trends, adjust your spending habits, and make informed decisions about saving and investing.

Together, understanding your net worth and cash flow will empower you to create a solid financial plan that aligns with your early retirement goals. By regularly evaluating these metrics, you can make necessary adjustments to your income, spending, and saving strategies, ultimately paving the way to a more secure financial future.

Identifying Areas For Improvement

Once you have a clear understanding of your income, expenses, net worth, and cash flow, the next step is to identify areas for improvement in your financial situation. This process involves analyzing your current habits, recognizing inefficiencies, and pinpointing specific changes that can enhance your financial stability and support your early retirement goals.

Start by reviewing your expenses in detail. Categorize them into needs (essential living costs such as housing, food, and utilities) and wants (discretionary spending like dining out, entertainment, and luxury items). This analysis can help you see where you might be overspending and highlight opportunities to cut back. Consider implementing strategies such as adopting a more frugal lifestyle or seeking alternatives for expensive habits. Small changes can accumulate significantly over time, contributing to your savings.

Next, evaluate your income sources. Are there opportunities for advancement in your current job, or could you pursue additional income streams? This could involve asking for a raise, seeking a promotion, or exploring side gigs that align with your skills and interests. Diversifying your income can create a more stable financial foundation and accelerate your path toward early retirement.

Another important aspect to consider is your saving and investment strategies. Review your current savings rate and investment portfolio to determine if you are on track to meet your financial goals. If your savings rate is low or your investments are not diversified, it may be time to develop a more aggressive savings plan or consult with a financial advisor to optimize your investment choices.

Lastly, reflect on your overall financial mindset and habits. Are you setting specific financial goals and monitoring your progress toward achieving them? Cultivating a proactive approach to managing your finances will empower you to make informed decisions and stay focused on your path to early retirement.

By systematically identifying and addressing these areas for improvement, you can create a more effective financial strategy that aligns with your aspirations for early retirement. Taking actionable steps today will build a strong foundation for a secure and fulfilling future.

CHAPTER 3: THE FIRE MOVEMENT

The Fire Movement

The FIRE movement, which stands for Financial Independence, Retire Early, is a lifestyle philosophy that emphasizes saving and investing aggressively to achieve financial independence at a young age. The core idea is to accumulate enough wealth to live off the returns of your investments, allowing you to retire much earlier than the traditional retirement age. The FIRE movement has gained popularity in recent years, appealing to those who seek greater freedom and control over their lives, free from the constraints of a nine-to-five job.

At the heart of the FIRE philosophy is a commitment to frugality and intentional living. Proponents advocate for reducing expenses significantly, often by making lifestyle changes that prioritize long-term financial goals over short-term pleasures. This could include downsizing housing, minimizing discretionary spending, or embracing minimalism. By focusing on saving a high percentage of their income—often 50% or more—individuals can build a substantial investment portfolio that supports their desired lifestyle without the need for traditional employment.

Within the FIRE movement, there are various approaches that cater to different preferences and lifestyles. Lean FIRE focuses on achieving financial independence with a minimalist lifestyle, allowing individuals to live on a very tight budget. This approach often emphasizes extreme frugality and a significant reduction in living expenses. In contrast, Fat FIRE allows for a more comfortable lifestyle post-retirement, requiring a larger investment portfolio to support higher spending. Those pursuing Fat FIRE typically aim for a higher savings rate to ensure they can enjoy a more luxurious retirement.

Barista FIRE is another variant that appeals to those who desire a balance between work and leisure. Individuals pursuing Barista FIRE might choose to work part-time or take on a job with less stress to supplement their income after achieving financial independence. This approach enables them to enjoy their newfound freedom while still contributing to their financial well-being.

Real-life success stories of those who have achieved FIRE serve as inspiration for others on this journey. Many individuals share their experiences through blogs, podcasts, and social media, detailing their paths to financial independence. These stories often highlight the challenges faced, the sacrifices made, and the ultimate rewards of living life on their own terms. Whether it's a couple who downsized their home and embraced a nomadic lifestyle or a single professional who invested wisely and retired in their thirties, these narratives resonate with those looking to transform their financial future.

The FIRE movement offers a compelling alternative to the conventional work-life balance, encouraging individuals to take control of their finances and design a life that aligns with their values and aspirations. By understanding the principles of FIRE and exploring the various approaches, you can determine which path resonates with you and embark on your journey toward financial independence and early retirement.

Different Approaches To Fire

The FIRE movement is not a one-size-fits-all philosophy; it encompasses various approaches that cater to different lifestyles, financial goals, and personal values. Understanding these different paths can help you determine which strategy aligns best with your aspirations for financial independence and early retirement.

Lean FIRE is the most frugal approach within the FIRE movement. Individuals pursuing Lean FIRE focus on drastically reducing their living expenses to achieve financial independence as quickly as possible. This often involves living a minimalist lifestyle, which may include downsizing to a smaller home, eliminating non-essential expenses, and embracing simple living principles. Those who choose Lean FIRE are typically very disciplined about their spending and prioritize saving a significant portion of their income—often 50% or more. While the Lean FIRE lifestyle can be rewarding, it may require some sacrifices in terms of comfort and leisure.

On the opposite end of the spectrum is Fat FIRE, which allows for a more comfortable lifestyle during retirement. People pursuing Fat FIRE aim to accumulate a larger investment portfolio to support higher living expenses. This approach often appeals to those who want to maintain their current standard of living or enjoy more luxuries in retirement, such as travel, dining out, and engaging in hobbies. Fat FIRE requires saving a substantial amount of money —usually in the range of 25 to 30 times one's annual expenses —allowing for a more lavish lifestyle post-retirement. Those who pursue this route often find a balance between aggressive savings and enjoying their income.

Barista FIRE is a hybrid approach that appeals to those who want to enjoy the benefits of financial independence while still engaging in part-time work. Individuals who follow the Barista FIRE model might choose to work in a low-stress job that covers a portion of their expenses while allowing them ample free time to pursue personal interests and passions. This approach offers a compromise between the extremes of Lean and Fat FIRE, enabling individuals to enjoy a more comfortable lifestyle while maintaining some income. It also provides a social outlet and a sense of purpose, which can be important for mental well-being.

Coast FIRE is another emerging strategy that allows individuals to reach a point where they can "coast" toward financial independence without aggressive saving in the later years of their careers. Those pursuing Coast FIRE typically save enough early in their careers to ensure they can retire comfortably without needing to save aggressively later on. This strategy emphasizes the power of compound interest and allows for a more relaxed approach to saving in mid-career, enabling individuals to focus on other aspects of life, such as career fulfillment or personal development.

Each of these approaches to FIRE offers unique benefits and challenges, allowing individuals to tailor their journey to their specific needs and circumstances. By understanding these different paths, you can make informed decisions about your financial future, ensuring that your approach to financial independence aligns with your goals, values, and desired lifestyle.

CHAPTER 4: SETTING FINANCIAL GOALS

Establishing Short And Long-Term Financial Objectives

Setting clear financial goals is essential for successfully navigating the path to early retirement. By establishing both short-term and long-term objectives, you create a roadmap that guides your decisions and keeps you focused on your aspirations.

Short-term financial goals are typically objectives you aim to achieve within the next one to three years. These goals often include practical steps that contribute to your overall financial health and prepare you for early retirement. Examples of short-term goals may include building an emergency fund, paying off high-interest debt, or saving for a specific purchase, such as a vacation or home renovation. These goals should be specific, measurable, attainable, relevant, and time-bound (SMART) to provide clarity and direction.

On the other hand, long-term financial goals encompass your aspirations for retirement and beyond, generally spanning three years or more. These objectives often involve larger financial milestones, such as accumulating a certain amount of retirement savings, achieving a specific net worth, or creating passive income streams through investments. When setting long-term goals, it's essential to envision what financial independence means for you and to outline the steps necessary to reach that vision. This may include setting benchmarks for savings rates, investment returns, and other financial metrics that align with your retirement plans.

Establishing both short and long-term objectives helps create a cohesive strategy that can adapt over time. It's essential to regularly review and adjust your goals as your circumstances change or as you gain new insights into your financial journey. Life can present unexpected challenges and opportunities, so maintaining flexibility in your goal-setting is crucial. Being open to modifying your objectives based on your evolving needs allows you to stay on track while also accommodating new aspirations that may arise along the way.

In summary, the foundation of your early retirement plan lies in the clear articulation of both short-term and long-term financial goals. By establishing these objectives, you not only enhance your focus and motivation but also create a solid framework that guides your decisions and actions as you work toward the freedom and lifestyle you envision in your retirement years.

Creating A Vision For Your Retirement

Crafting a clear vision for your retirement is an essential step toward achieving early retirement. This vision serves as your guiding star, providing direction and purpose as you navigate your financial journey. By envisioning your ideal retirement lifestyle, you can make informed decisions that align with your goals and values.

Start by reflecting on what you truly want from your retirement. Consider the activities, experiences, and environments that resonate with you. Do you envision traveling the world, starting a new business, volunteering, or spending more time with family? Take the time to write down your thoughts, creating a vivid picture of how you want to spend your days once you retire. This vision should encompass not only how you will fill your time but also the kind of lifestyle you wish to maintain—whether it's a modest, frugal lifestyle or one that includes more luxurious experiences.

Next, think about the financial aspects that will support your vision. Assess the costs associated with the lifestyle you desire. This may include travel expenses, housing, healthcare, hobbies, and other activities that are important to you. Understanding these costs will help you set realistic financial goals that align with your vision. You might find it useful to create a retirement budget that estimates your monthly and annual expenses, ensuring that you can sustain your desired lifestyle without financial strain.

In addition to the practical elements, consider the emotional and psychological aspects of retirement. What kind of legacy do you want to leave? How do you want to contribute to your community or the world at large? These considerations can enrich your vision, providing a sense of fulfillment and purpose beyond just financial security.

Lastly, visualize your retirement as a dynamic and evolving phase of life. Be open to the idea that your vision may change over time as you gain new experiences and insights. Regularly revisiting and refining your vision will keep it aligned with your evolving values and desires, ensuring that your path remains relevant and motivating.

In summary, creating a vision for your retirement is a foundational step in your journey toward early retirement. By articulating your dreams and aspirations, you establish a clear framework for your financial goals and decision-making. This vision not only clarifies what you want to achieve but also inspires and motivates you to take the necessary steps to turn those dreams into reality.

Importance Of Flexibility In Goal Setting

Setting financial goals is crucial for achieving early retirement, but equally important is the ability to remain flexible as circumstances change. Life is inherently unpredictable, and being adaptable in your goal-setting can mean the difference between staying on track and feeling overwhelmed when obstacles arise.

Flexibility allows you to adjust your goals in response to changing financial situations, personal priorities, or unexpected challenges. For instance, you may experience a job loss, a significant medical expense, or shifts in your family dynamics that impact your income or spending habits. In such cases, having a flexible mindset can help you reassess your objectives and modify your plans accordingly. Rather than viewing setbacks as failures, consider them opportunities to refine your goals and develop alternative strategies that still align with your vision of retirement.

Moreover, flexibility enables you to take advantage of new opportunities that may arise. As you progress toward your retirement goals, you may discover innovative investment options, side gigs, or lifestyle adjustments that can accelerate your journey. By remaining open to change, you can pivot and adapt your plans to incorporate these beneficial elements, enhancing your overall strategy.

Another key aspect of flexibility is recognizing that your priorities may evolve over time. What seems important today may shift as you gain new experiences or insights. For example, your initial goal might focus on accumulating wealth, but over time, you may find that work-life balance, community involvement, or pursuing passions takes precedence. Regularly revisiting your goals allows you to ensure they remain aligned with your current values and desires.

Additionally, being flexible with your goals fosters resilience and reduces stress. Rigid goals can lead to feelings of failure or frustration when circumstances do not go as planned. By adopting a more adaptable approach, you can cultivate a healthier relationship with your financial journey, viewing challenges as part of the process rather than insurmountable barriers.

In conclusion, flexibility in goal-setting is essential for navigating the complexities of financial planning for early retirement. It empowers you to respond to life's uncertainties, seize new opportunities, and ensure your goals reflect your evolving values. By embracing a flexible mindset, you can maintain momentum on your path to financial freedom while adapting to whatever life may bring your way.

CHAPTER 5: BUDGETING FOR EARLY RETIREMENT

Developing A Frugal Budget

Creating a frugal budget is a cornerstone of preparing for early retirement, as it enables you to maximize your savings while still enjoying a fulfilling lifestyle. A frugal budget focuses on prioritizing essential expenses and setting aside a significant portion of your income for savings and investments, all while ensuring you do not feel deprived in the process.

To start, assess your current income and identify your fixed and variable expenses. Fixed expenses include rent or mortgage payments, utilities, insurance, and loan repayments—costs that remain largely consistent each month. Variable expenses, on the other hand, can fluctuate and may include groceries, entertainment, dining out, and other discretionary spending. By understanding where your money goes, you can create a clear picture of your financial landscape.

Once you have a comprehensive view of your expenses, categorize them into essentials and non-essentials. Essentials are those necessary for your daily life, such as housing, food, transportation, and healthcare. Non-essentials may include entertainment, luxury items, or subscriptions. This categorization allows you to see where you can cut back. For instance, while you may need a roof over your head, you might find opportunities to save on non-essential spending, such as dining out or subscription services.

Next, set specific savings goals within your budget. Determine how much you want to save each month and consider establishing an automatic transfer to a savings or investment account as soon as you receive your income. Treating savings as a non-negotiable expense ensures that you prioritize it just like any other bill.

When developing a frugal budget, aim for a balance between saving aggressively and enjoying life. Look for ways to cut costs without compromising your quality of life. This might involve cooking at home instead of dining out, exploring free or low-cost recreational activities, or shopping during sales. By finding frugal alternatives to your usual spending habits, you can significantly reduce expenses while still having fun.

Moreover, consider employing the "50/30/20" rule as a guideline for your budget. This rule suggests allocating 50% of your income to necessities, 30% to discretionary spending, and 20% to savings. Adjust these percentages according to your personal goals and financial situation, but the general principle remains the same: prioritize saving while maintaining a balanced approach to spending.

Lastly, regularly review and adjust your budget as necessary. Financial situations can change due to unexpected expenses, income fluctuations, or lifestyle changes. Being flexible allows you to adapt your budget to current realities while still keeping your long-term retirement goals in sight.

In conclusion, developing a frugal budget is essential for anyone aiming for early retirement. By focusing on prioritizing savings, cutting non-essential expenses, and maintaining a balanced lifestyle, you can create a sustainable financial plan that supports your journey toward financial independence. With careful planning and commitment, a frugal budget can set the stage for achieving your retirement dreams.

Strategies For Cutting Expenses

Cutting expenses is a vital step toward achieving early retirement, as it allows you to save more money and allocate resources more effectively. By adopting some strategic approaches, you can reduce your spending without sacrificing your quality of life.

First, start with a thorough review of your monthly expenses. Categorize them into fixed and variable costs to identify where your money is going. Fixed costs, such as housing and insurance, are harder to adjust but can sometimes be renegotiated or refined. For example, consider shopping around for better rates on insurance or exploring options for refinancing your mortgage. Variable expenses, however, are more flexible and offer numerous opportunities for reduction.

One of the most effective strategies for cutting costs is to examine your discretionary spending. This includes categories like dining out, entertainment, and subscriptions. Evaluate how often you eat at restaurants or order takeout, and try to reduce those expenses by cooking at home. Meal planning not only saves money but also allows for healthier eating. Similarly, consider cutting back on entertainment costs by seeking out free local events, enjoying nature, or hosting game nights with friends instead of expensive outings.

Subscriptions can also accumulate quickly and often go unnoticed. Review all your subscription services, from streaming platforms to magazine subscriptions, and determine which ones you truly use. Cancel any that you can live without or consider sharing subscriptions with friends or family to split costs.

Another effective strategy is to embrace minimalism in your purchasing habits. Before making a purchase, ask yourself if it is a need or a want. Consider implementing a waiting period for non-essential purchases—this gives you time to think about whether you really need the item. Additionally, focus on buying quality items that last longer, which can ultimately save money over time compared to cheaper, disposable alternatives.

Utilizing technology can also aid in cutting expenses. There are numerous budgeting and expense-tracking apps that help you monitor your spending habits and identify areas for improvement. Many apps can provide insights into your spending patterns, making it easier to pinpoint where you can cut back.

Transportation costs are another significant area where savings can be realized. If you own a vehicle, consider using public transportation, carpooling, or biking whenever possible. These alternatives can save you money on gas, maintenance, and parking fees. Additionally, if you find that you are not using your car frequently, you might explore options like car-sharing services or even selling the vehicle altogether.

Finally, don't underestimate the power of negotiating bills. Many companies are willing to discuss rates, especially if you are a loyal customer. Whether it's your cable provider, internet service, or phone bill, reaching out to inquire about discounts or promotions can result in significant savings.

By implementing these strategies for cutting expenses, you can create a more financially sustainable lifestyle that supports your goal of early retirement. With mindful spending, careful planning, and a willingness to make adjustments, you'll find that saving money can also lead to a more fulfilling and intentional way of living.

Tools And Apps For Effective Budgeting

In today's digital age, various tools and apps can help you manage your finances more effectively and stay on track with your budgeting goals. Utilizing these resources can simplify the budgeting process, making it easier to track your spending, save money, and achieve your early retirement objectives.

One of the most popular types of budgeting tools is personal finance apps. These apps allow you to connect your bank accounts, credit cards, and investment accounts to provide a comprehensive view of your financial situation. Apps like Mint, YNAB (You Need a Budget), and PocketGuard automatically categorize your transactions, giving you insights into where your money is going. This real-time tracking can help you identify spending habits that may need adjustment and encourage more mindful financial decisions.

YNAB, in particular, is known for its proactive approach to budgeting. It encourages users to allocate every dollar they earn to specific categories, which fosters a habit of prioritizing savings and expenses. The app also offers educational resources to help you understand the principles of budgeting better.

Another effective tool is expense tracking software. Apps like Expensify or Personal Capital allow you to log and categorize your expenses, making it easier to see where you can cut back. These tools often include features for generating reports, which can provide valuable insights into your spending patterns over time. By regularly reviewing these reports, you can spot trends and make informed decisions about future expenditures.

If you prefer a more hands-on approach, spreadsheet programs like Microsoft Excel or Google Sheets can be excellent for creating custom budgets. Templates are readily available online, allowing you to set up a budgeting framework that suits your specific needs. By manually entering your income and expenses, you gain a deeper understanding of your financial situation. This method also enables you to tailor your budget as your financial circumstances change.

For those who want to track their progress visually, goal-setting apps such as Qapital or SmartyPig can be motivating. These apps allow you to set savings goals and visualize your progress, which can be a powerful incentive to stay disciplined in your saving efforts. By gamifying the saving process, these tools can make budgeting feel less like a chore and more like an achievement.

Another valuable resource is financial community platforms like EveryDollar or GoodBudget, which encourage users to share tips and strategies for budgeting and saving. Engaging with a community can provide support, motivation, and accountability, making it easier to stay committed to your financial goals.

Lastly, remember to leverage reminders and alerts. Many budgeting apps allow you to set notifications for upcoming bills or when you approach spending limits in certain categories. These alerts can help you avoid late fees and keep you mindful of your budget throughout the month.

By incorporating these tools and apps into your financial routine, you can streamline the budgeting process and stay organized. Effective budgeting is not just about tracking numbers; it's about fostering habits that lead to financial stability and success. With the right resources at your fingertips, you'll be better equipped to make informed decisions, cut unnecessary expenses, and ultimately achieve your goal of early retirement.

CHAPTER 6: INCREASING INCOME FOR EARLY RETIREMENT

Exploring Side Hustles And Freelance Opportunities

In the pursuit of early retirement, increasing your income is a vital strategy, and one of the most effective ways to achieve this is by exploring side hustles and freelance opportunities. Side hustles not only provide additional financial resources but also allow you to pursue passions, develop new skills, and potentially turn hobbies into profitable ventures.

The first step in finding a suitable side hustle is to assess your skills, interests, and availability. Think about what you enjoy doing in your spare time or what expertise you possess. For instance, if you have a knack for writing, consider freelance writing or blogging. If you enjoy graphic design, platforms like Fiverr or Upwork can connect you with clients looking for design work. Similarly, if you have expertise in a specific field, consulting or coaching can be a lucrative option. Identifying your strengths and interests can help you choose a side hustle that is both enjoyable and financially rewarding.

Many people find success in the gig economy, which offers various flexible work opportunities. Apps and websites like Uber, DoorDash, or TaskRabbit enable you to earn money on your schedule, whether it's driving, delivering food, or completing household tasks. These platforms are excellent for individuals looking to earn extra income without a long-term commitment.

In addition to gig work, consider leveraging your existing network to find freelance opportunities. Let friends, family, and colleagues know that you're available for side projects. Word-of-mouth can lead to unexpected opportunities, whether it's helping a neighbor with home repairs, babysitting, or providing tutoring in a subject you excel at.

If you're looking to develop a more structured side business, e-commerce can be a promising avenue. Selling products online through platforms like Etsy, eBay, or Amazon allows you to reach a broader audience. Whether you create handmade crafts, sell vintage items, or source products for resale, e-commerce can turn a passion into profit.

Moreover, teaching and sharing knowledge is another way to generate income. If you possess expertise in a particular area, consider offering online courses or workshops. Platforms like Teachable or Skillshare make it easy to create and sell courses on topics you are passionate about, from cooking to photography to personal finance.

Finally, remember that while side hustles can significantly boost your income, they require time and effort. It's essential to balance your side work with your primary job and personal life. Setting clear goals and maintaining organization can help you manage your time effectively.

Exploring side hustles not only increases your income but also enhances your skills and provides valuable experiences that can contribute to your professional growth. By diversifying your income streams through these various opportunities, you can take meaningful steps toward achieving your early retirement goals while enjoying the journey along the way.

Investing In Yourself: Education And Skill Development

Investing in yourself through education and skill development is a crucial component of increasing your income and paving the way to early retirement. By enhancing your skills and expanding your knowledge, you not only make yourself more marketable but also increase your potential for higher earnings, whether through your current job or side ventures.

One of the most effective ways to invest in yourself is by pursuing further education. This doesn't necessarily mean going back to traditional school; there are numerous options available, from online courses to workshops and certification programs. Many platforms, such as Coursera, Udemy, and LinkedIn Learning, offer a wide range of courses on various subjects, often taught by industry experts. Whether you're looking to learn a new programming language, improve your writing skills, or delve into digital marketing, these resources provide flexible learning opportunities that fit your schedule and budget.

In addition to formal courses, consider attending seminars, webinars, and industry conferences. These events not only provide valuable insights and knowledge but also offer networking opportunities that can lead to new job prospects or collaborations. Engaging with professionals in your field can open doors to mentorship, partnerships, and other avenues for growth.

Skill development is equally important. Identify the skills that are in demand in your industry and focus on acquiring or enhancing them. This could be anything from mastering software tools to improving your communication abilities. Practical experience is often the best teacher, so look for ways to apply new skills in real-world settings. Volunteer for projects at work, take on freelance assignments, or participate in community initiatives that allow you to practice and refine your skills.

Furthermore, soft skills such as leadership, negotiation, and emotional intelligence are increasingly valued in the workplace. Consider workshops or coaching sessions focused on these areas, as they can significantly enhance your professional relationships and career advancement prospects.

Another powerful way to invest in yourself is by building a personal brand. This involves creating a professional online presence that showcases your skills and achievements. Use platforms like LinkedIn to connect with others in your field, share your knowledge through articles or posts, and actively participate in discussions. A strong personal brand can lead to new job opportunities and increase your credibility in your industry.

Finally, remember that investing in yourself is a lifelong journey. Regularly assess your skills, set new learning goals, and stay informed about industry trends. Embrace a mindset of continuous improvement, and be open to adapting as your career and interests evolve.

By prioritizing education and skill development, you equip yourself with the tools necessary to increase your income, advance in your career, and ultimately achieve your goal of early retirement. Investing in yourself is not just a financial decision; it's an investment in your future, enhancing your potential and helping you create the life you desire.

The Benefits Of Passive Income Streams

Passive income streams are a powerful way to bolster your financial stability and accelerate your journey toward early retirement. Unlike traditional income, which typically requires active participation, passive income allows you to earn money with minimal ongoing effort. This financial strategy can significantly enhance your overall wealth-building potential and provide several distinct advantages.

One of the most compelling benefits of passive income is the ability to generate revenue while you focus on other pursuits. Whether you're working full-time, pursuing a side hustle, or enjoying leisure activities, passive income streams work for you behind the scenes. This can free up valuable time and mental energy, allowing you to concentrate on what truly matters to you —be it your career, family, or personal interests.

Another significant advantage is the potential for financial security. By diversifying your income sources, you create a safety net that can help you weather economic uncertainties. If your primary income source fluctuates or diminishes, having passive income can provide a buffer, reducing stress and giving you peace of mind. This stability is especially crucial as you approach retirement, ensuring you have funds available when you need them most.

Moreover, passive income can contribute to a more comfortable lifestyle. The additional funds can be used to enhance your quality of life, whether it's traveling, indulging in hobbies, or simply enjoying more leisure time. This financial freedom allows you to spend your days in ways that align with your values and aspirations, rather than being confined by financial limitations.

Creating passive income streams can also accelerate your savings and investment efforts. The money earned from these sources can be reinvested to grow your wealth further. Whether you choose to invest in real estate, stocks, or start a business, reinvesting your passive income can compound your returns, putting you on a faster track to financial independence.

There's also the added benefit of building assets. Many passive income streams, such as rental properties or dividend-generating investments, can appreciate in value over time. This means that not only are you earning money passively, but you're also increasing your overall net worth. As you accumulate assets, you create a solid foundation for your future financial security.

Lastly, establishing passive income streams can empower you to take more control over your financial destiny. It encourages you to think creatively about how to leverage your skills, knowledge, and resources. From creating online courses and writing e-books to investing in peer-to-peer lending or affiliate marketing, the possibilities for generating passive income are vast and can be tailored to suit your interests and expertise.

In summary, passive income streams offer a myriad of benefits that align perfectly with the goals of early retirement. They provide financial security, enhance your quality of life, accelerate your wealth-building efforts, and empower you to take control of your financial future. By exploring and establishing these income sources, you can create a more sustainable and fulfilling path toward achieving your early retirement dreams.

CHAPTER 7: SAVING AND INVESTING WISELY

Importance Of High Savings Rates And Investment Growth

Achieving early retirement requires not only careful planning but also a robust approach to saving and investing. One of the cornerstones of this strategy is maintaining a high savings rate, which directly impacts your ability to accumulate wealth and secure financial freedom. A higher savings rate allows you to build a substantial nest egg more quickly, enabling you to transition into retirement at an earlier age.

The relationship between savings rates and investment growth is significant. When you save a larger percentage of your income, you have more capital to invest. This increased capital can then be allocated to various investment vehicles that offer the potential for growth. Over time, the power of compound interest can transform even modest investments into substantial wealth. By consistently saving and reinvesting your returns, you harness the exponential growth potential that compound interest provides, multiplying your savings as time goes on.

Moreover, a high savings rate acts as a buffer against unexpected expenses or economic downturns. When you have a solid financial cushion, you are less likely to panic during market fluctuations or financial crises. This stability enables you to stick to your long-term investment strategy without making impulsive decisions based on short-term market volatility.

In addition to savings, understanding the importance of investment growth is crucial for building wealth. Investment growth not only helps to offset inflation but also allows your money to work for you. By investing wisely, you can achieve returns that significantly outpace traditional savings accounts, which often yield minimal interest. This growth is essential for reaching your financial goals and ultimately retiring early.

Balancing your savings with a diversified investment portfolio can optimize your financial strategy. While high savings rates provide a solid foundation, investments can amplify your wealth-building efforts. This synergy between saving and investing is vital for creating a sustainable financial future.

In conclusion, prioritizing a high savings rate and focusing on investment growth are fundamental to achieving early retirement. These practices not only build wealth but also foster financial security, allowing you to pursue your retirement dreams with confidence. By committing to a disciplined approach to saving and investing, you lay the groundwork for a prosperous and fulfilling future.

Overview Of Investment Options: Stocks, Bonds, And Real Estate

When planning for early retirement, it's crucial to understand the various investment options available to you. Each type of investment has its unique characteristics, risks, and potential returns. Here's a brief overview of three primary investment vehicles: stocks, bonds, and real estate.

Stocks represent ownership in a company. When you buy shares of a stock, you become a partial owner and have a claim on a portion of the company's assets and earnings. Stocks are generally considered high-risk investments but also offer the potential for high returns. Historically, the stock market has outperformed other asset classes over the long term, making it an attractive option for those looking to build wealth. However, stock prices can be volatile in the short term, which means that investors must be prepared for market fluctuations and a long-term investment horizon.

Bonds, on the other hand, are essentially loans that you provide to a company or government. When you purchase a bond, you're lending money in exchange for periodic interest payments and the return of the bond's face value at maturity. Bonds are generally considered safer than stocks, as they offer more predictable income and lower volatility. However, they typically provide lower returns compared to stocks. The balance between stocks and bonds in your portfolio can help manage risk while still seeking growth, depending on your financial goals and risk tolerance.

Real estate is another popular investment option, providing both potential income and appreciation. Investing in real estate can take various forms, including residential properties, commercial real estate, or real estate investment trusts (REITs). Real estate can generate income through rental payments and may appreciate over time, contributing to your overall wealth. However, it also requires a significant initial investment and ongoing management. Real estate markets can fluctuate, and unexpected expenses—like maintenance or vacancies—can impact profitability.

Each of these investment options has its own set of advantages and challenges. As you develop your investment strategy for early retirement, consider your risk tolerance, investment goals, and time horizon. A diversified portfolio that combines stocks, bonds, and real estate can help mitigate risks and maximize growth potential, setting you on the path toward achieving financial independence and early retirement. By understanding the unique features of each asset class, you can make informed decisions that align with your financial objectives.

Understanding Risk Tolerance

Understanding your risk tolerance is a critical aspect of developing a successful investment strategy, especially when planning for early retirement. Risk tolerance refers to your ability and willingness to endure fluctuations in the value of your investments without becoming overly stressed or making impulsive decisions. It encompasses both psychological factors—how you feel about risk—and financial factors—how much risk you can afford to take based on your financial situation.

Several factors influence your risk tolerance. First, consider your investment time horizon. The longer you have to invest before you need to access your funds, the more risk you can generally afford to take. Younger investors, for instance, typically have a longer time horizon, allowing them to ride out market fluctuations. Conversely, if you plan to retire soon or need your investments for a specific purpose within a short timeframe, a more conservative approach may be warranted.

Your financial situation also plays a crucial role in determining risk tolerance. Take stock of your income, expenses, debts, and savings. If you have a stable income and a solid emergency fund, you may feel more comfortable taking on higher-risk investments. On the other hand, if you are living paycheck to paycheck or have significant financial obligations, a more cautious strategy may be appropriate.

Emotional factors can further complicate your relationship with risk. Some individuals thrive on the excitement of market volatility, while others may experience anxiety at the thought of losing money. It's essential to be honest with yourself about how you react to market changes. A good way to gauge your emotional response to risk is to consider how you would feel if your investments dropped by 20% in a short period. Would you stay the course, or would you feel compelled to sell and potentially lock in losses?

Finally, it's helpful to assess your investment knowledge and experience. New investors may be more apprehensive about risk, while seasoned investors might be more comfortable navigating volatility based on their past experiences.

To effectively determine your risk tolerance, consider taking a risk assessment questionnaire, which can help you clarify your feelings and preferences regarding risk. Many financial advisors offer these tools, or you can find them online. Understanding your risk tolerance will enable you to create an investment portfolio that aligns with your financial goals, ensuring that you can pursue early retirement while maintaining peace of mind about your investment strategy.

CHAPTER 8: PLANNING FOR HEALTHCARE AND INSURANCE

Navigating Healthcare Costs In Early Retirement

Navigating healthcare costs in early retirement can be one of the most significant financial challenges you will face. As you transition from a regular paycheck to a fixed income, understanding how to manage and anticipate these expenses is essential for maintaining your financial health. The need for healthcare often increases with age, and being proactive about these costs can help you avoid unexpected financial burdens.

First, it's important to understand that Medicare eligibility typically begins at age 65, so if you retire before this age, you will need to find alternative health insurance coverage. You might consider options such as private health insurance plans, employer-sponsored coverage (if available), or plans offered through the Affordable Care Act (ACA) marketplace. Each option comes with its own costs, benefits, and limitations, so it's crucial to compare these carefully to find a plan that meets your needs.

In addition to premiums, be aware of other costs associated with healthcare, including deductibles, copayments, and out-of-pocket maximums. Familiarizing yourself with these terms will help you assess the overall affordability of a health insurance plan. Additionally, consider the network of providers and hospitals associated with your insurance. Staying in-network can significantly reduce your costs, so if you have preferred healthcare providers, ensure they are covered under the plan you choose.

Another critical aspect of healthcare in early retirement is the potential need for long-term care. This type of care can be expensive and is often not covered by standard health insurance or Medicare. Planning for long-term care involves understanding your options, such as purchasing long-term care insurance or exploring alternatives like home care services or assisted living facilities. Assessing your potential needs early can help you make informed decisions and budget accordingly.

Creating a healthcare budget is vital in navigating these costs. Start by estimating your annual healthcare expenses based on your current situation and any known medical needs. Include costs such as insurance premiums, routine medical expenses, prescription medications, and anticipated long-term care needs. Factor in the possibility of unexpected medical emergencies, which can have a significant impact on your finances. It may also be wise to set aside a separate emergency fund specifically for healthcare-related expenses.

In conclusion, navigating healthcare costs in early retirement requires careful planning and consideration. By understanding your insurance options, preparing for long-term care, and creating a detailed healthcare budget, you can minimize stress and ensure that your health needs are met without jeopardizing your financial security. Taking these proactive steps will empower you to enjoy your retirement with peace of mind, knowing that you are prepared for the health challenges that may arise.

Importance Of Health Insurance And Long-Term Care Planning

Health insurance is a critical component of financial security in early retirement. As medical expenses can quickly accumulate, having adequate coverage ensures that you are protected from potentially devastating costs. Even healthy individuals can encounter unexpected health issues or accidents, making it essential to have a reliable insurance plan in place. Without health insurance, a single medical emergency can lead to overwhelming debt and financial instability.

When planning for health insurance, it's important to evaluate the various options available to early retirees. This includes private insurance plans, COBRA continuation coverage from a previous employer, and plans available through the Affordable Care Act (ACA) marketplace. Each option varies in terms of coverage, cost, and eligibility requirements. Carefully reviewing these plans helps you choose one that aligns with your healthcare needs and budget.

Moreover, understanding the nuances of your chosen plan—such as premiums, deductibles, copays, and out-of-pocket maximums—can prevent unexpected financial burdens. Ensure that your plan covers the essential services you may need, including regular check-ups, prescription medications, and specialist visits.

Long-term care planning is another vital aspect of healthcare in retirement. As individuals age, the likelihood of needing assistance with daily activities increases. Long-term care encompasses a range of services, including home health care, assisted living, and nursing home care. Unfortunately, traditional health insurance and Medicare often do not cover these expenses, leaving a significant gap in financial protection.

To prepare for potential long-term care needs, consider purchasing long-term care insurance. This specialized coverage can help pay for services that support daily living, such as personal care, rehabilitation, or custodial care. The earlier you start planning for long-term care, the more options you will have, as age and health status can affect eligibility and premiums.

In addition to insurance, explore alternative strategies for long-term care planning, such as setting aside savings specifically for this purpose or considering state programs that offer assistance. Engaging in discussions with family members about potential care needs and preferences can also be beneficial, ensuring that everyone is on the same page.

In summary, having robust health insurance and a comprehensive long-term care plan is essential for safeguarding your financial well-being in early retirement. By proactively addressing these areas, you can mitigate the impact of unforeseen medical costs and ensure that you receive the care you need as you age. Being well-prepared not only protects your finances but also grants you peace of mind, allowing you to focus on enjoying your retirement years.

Creating A Healthcare Budget

Creating a healthcare budget is an essential step in preparing for early retirement, as it helps you anticipate and manage medical expenses effectively. A well-planned budget allows you to allocate resources for various healthcare needs, ensuring that you are not caught off guard by unexpected costs.

Start by gathering information about your current and projected healthcare expenses. This includes premiums for health insurance, out-of-pocket costs for doctor visits, prescriptions, preventive care, and any anticipated long-term care expenses. If you have ongoing medical conditions, factor in the costs of regular treatments, medications, and necessary supplies.

Next, determine your health insurance premiums based on the plan you choose for retirement. This can involve comparing different plans to find one that meets your needs while remaining affordable. Remember to account for any deductibles and copayments, as these can significantly impact your overall costs.

Once you have a clear picture of your current expenses, project your future healthcare needs. Consider potential changes in health status as you age, which may require more frequent medical visits or specialized care. It can be helpful to consult with your healthcare provider about possible future needs based on your medical history and lifestyle.

With this information in hand, create a monthly healthcare budget. Break down your expenses into categories, such as insurance premiums, out-of-pocket costs, medications, and preventive services. Be sure to leave some room for unexpected expenses, as medical situations can arise that were not initially planned for.

In addition to budgeting for direct healthcare costs, consider setting aside a separate fund for long-term care. This could be a savings account specifically designated for future care needs or a long-term care insurance policy. The earlier you start saving for this purpose, the more financially secure you will be.

Lastly, regularly review and adjust your healthcare budget as needed. Life circumstances, insurance plans, and health needs can change, so it's important to revisit your budget periodically to ensure it still aligns with your situation. Keeping an eye on your healthcare spending can help you identify areas where you can save and allow for necessary adjustments.

By creating a thoughtful and comprehensive healthcare budget, you can navigate the complexities of medical expenses in retirement with confidence. This proactive approach not only protects your finances but also enhances your overall well-being, enabling you to focus on enjoying your early retirement years without the stress of financial uncertainty.

CHAPTER 9: MAKING THE TRANSITION TO EARLY RETIREMENT

Preparing Mentally For Retirement

Transitioning to early retirement is as much a mental and emotional journey as it is a financial one. As you shift from a structured work life to a more flexible lifestyle, it's essential to prepare yourself for the changes that come with this significant life milestone. Understanding and addressing the psychological aspects of retirement can lead to a more fulfilling and enjoyable experience.

One of the primary challenges in retirement is the potential loss of identity and purpose. Many people derive a sense of self-worth and structure from their careers, and stepping away from that can lead to feelings of uncertainty or even anxiety. To combat this, it's crucial to reflect on your values and what you truly want from your retirement years. Consider what passions you might want to pursue, the activities you've always dreamed of trying, or the skills you've wanted to develop. By identifying these areas, you can start to cultivate a new sense of purpose outside of work.

Another important aspect of mental preparation is embracing the emotional adjustments that come with retirement. You may experience a mix of excitement and apprehension about this new chapter in your life. It's normal to feel a sense of loss for your working life and the daily interactions that came with it. Acknowledge these feelings and give yourself permission to process them. Journaling, talking with friends, or seeking support from a therapist can be helpful in navigating these emotions.

Establishing a routine in retirement can provide the structure and stability that may be lacking after leaving the workforce. Consider creating a daily schedule that includes a mix of activities, such as exercise, hobbies, volunteer work, or social engagements. Having a routine helps to maintain a sense of normalcy and gives you something to look forward to each day. Incorporating new hobbies can also provide opportunities for personal growth and fulfillment, allowing you to explore interests you may have put aside during your working years.

Maintaining social connections is another key factor in preparing for retirement. Your work environment often provides a built-in social network, and leaving that behind can lead to feelings of isolation. To counter this, be proactive in nurturing existing relationships and seeking out new ones. Joining clubs, attending community events, or participating in classes can help you meet like-minded individuals. Establishing regular social activities, whether it's a weekly coffee with friends or a monthly book club, can ensure you stay connected and engaged.

Lastly, consider the benefits of mental exercises and mindfulness practices. Engaging in activities such as meditation, yoga, or mindfulness can enhance your emotional well-being and help you adapt to the changes in your life. These practices can foster resilience and promote a positive mindset as you navigate the transition into retirement.

In conclusion, preparing mentally for early retirement involves reflection, planning, and a commitment to maintaining connections and routines. By addressing the psychological aspects of this transition, you can create a fulfilling and enriching retirement experience that aligns with your goals and aspirations. Embrace this opportunity to redefine your life and enjoy the freedom that early retirement brings.

Establishing A Retirement Routine And Hobbies

Establishing a fulfilling routine and engaging in hobbies are essential steps in creating a satisfying early retirement experience. With the newfound freedom from work obligations, it's important to design a structure that keeps you motivated and enriched, while also allowing for spontaneity and leisure.

First, consider what aspects of your pre-retirement routine you enjoyed and how you can adapt them to your new lifestyle. A daily schedule can provide a sense of purpose and direction. Start by outlining a basic framework for your week, incorporating time for activities you find enjoyable, fulfilling, and meaningful. This could include exercise, volunteering, social engagements, or even simple tasks like gardening or reading.

Physical activity is a crucial component of any retirement routine. Regular exercise not only helps maintain physical health but also improves mental well-being. Whether it's walking, biking, yoga, or joining a local gym, finding an activity you love can be invigorating. Consider participating in group classes or community sports to combine fitness with social interaction, making it both enjoyable and rewarding.

Hobbies can also play a significant role in enriching your retirement. This is the time to explore interests you may have set aside during your career or to try something entirely new. Whether it's painting, cooking, crafting, gardening, or learning a musical instrument, dedicating time to these passions can provide a sense of accomplishment and joy. Consider taking classes or joining local clubs related to your hobbies to deepen your skills and meet new friends who share your interests.

Volunteering is another meaningful way to fill your time and give back to your community. Many retirees find purpose in helping others, whether it's through mentoring, working with charities, or participating in local initiatives. This not only provides a sense of fulfillment but also helps maintain social connections and combats feelings of isolation.

It's also important to allow for flexibility in your routine. While having a structured plan is beneficial, be open to spontaneity and new opportunities. Some days may call for relaxation, while others may present unexpected adventures. Embracing this balance can enhance your overall satisfaction and enjoyment in retirement.

Finally, keep in mind the significance of maintaining social interactions within your routine. Schedule regular meet-ups with friends or family, whether it's for a weekly coffee, game night, or shared activities. These connections are vital for emotional well-being and help create a rich social life during retirement.

In conclusion, establishing a routine and incorporating hobbies in retirement is crucial for maintaining a sense of purpose and fulfillment. By thoughtfully designing your days around activities you love and creating opportunities for social engagement, you can enjoy a rewarding and vibrant retirement that reflects your interests and passions.

Maintaining Social Connections

As you transition into early retirement, maintaining social connections becomes essential for emotional well-being and a fulfilling lifestyle. The shift from a structured work environment to a more flexible routine can sometimes lead to feelings of isolation, so it's important to actively nurture relationships that provide support, companionship, and joy.

One effective way to maintain social connections is to prioritize regular interactions with friends and family. Schedule weekly or monthly gatherings, whether it's a simple coffee date, a game night, or a shared meal. Making these get-togethers a routine can foster a sense of community and keep you engaged with loved ones. Additionally, consider reaching out to former colleagues; they can provide a familiar social network and an opportunity to reminisce about shared experiences.

Joining clubs or groups that align with your interests can also enhance your social life. Whether it's a book club, a hiking group, a crafting circle, or a gardening club, participating in activities you enjoy will introduce you to like-minded individuals. These connections can grow into meaningful friendships as you bond over shared passions and hobbies.

Volunteering is another powerful way to expand your social circle while making a positive impact. Many organizations seek out volunteers, providing opportunities to meet people while contributing to causes that matter to you. Not only does this help combat feelings of loneliness, but it can also instill a sense of purpose as you engage with your community.

Embracing technology can be beneficial in maintaining social connections, especially if you have friends or family living far away. Video calls, social media platforms, and messaging apps can help you stay in touch regularly. Organizing virtual gatherings or sharing updates online can keep relationships strong, regardless of physical distance.

As you cultivate these social connections, it's important to remain open to new friendships. Attend local events, workshops, or classes where you can meet new people and expand your social network. Being approachable and engaging in conversations can lead to unexpected connections and enrich your retirement experience.

Lastly, don't underestimate the value of being proactive in nurturing your relationships. Take the initiative to check in with friends and family, whether through a simple text, a phone call, or an invitation to meet up. Showing genuine interest in others' lives can deepen your connections and reinforce the importance of these relationships in your life.

In summary, maintaining social connections during early retirement is vital for your overall happiness and well-being. By prioritizing regular interactions, exploring new opportunities for social engagement, and being proactive in nurturing relationships, you can build a vibrant social network that enhances your retirement experience and provides lasting fulfillment.

CONCLUSION

As you reflect on the journey toward early retirement, it's important to revisit the key principles that can guide you along the way. Understanding the significance of financial planning, setting clear goals, and embracing a frugal mindset are foundational steps that can lead you to achieve the lifestyle you desire. Throughout this book, we've explored the importance of assessing your financial situation, leveraging the FIRE movement, and implementing effective budgeting strategies. Each of these components plays a vital role in building a path to financial independence.

As you consider your next steps, remember that actionable progress is crucial. Whether it's refining your budget, exploring new income streams, or investing wisely, every small decision contributes to your long-term goals. Embrace the opportunities available to you, and don't hesitate to seek out resources that can aid your journey.

However, as you pursue your aspirations, it's essential to recognize that the journey itself is as important as the destination. Each milestone you reach offers valuable lessons and experiences that enrich your life beyond mere financial success. Embrace the process of growth, learning, and discovery that comes with planning for your future.

By prioritizing your well-being, building strong social connections, and remaining flexible in your goals, you will not only work toward early retirement but also cultivate a fulfilling and meaningful life. Your path to financial independence is uniquely

www.ingramcontent.com/pod-product-compliance
Lightning Source LLC
Chambersburg PA
CBHW070946220526
45471CB00007B/2920